Frog or Toad?

by Lucy Floyd

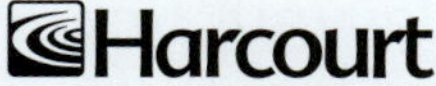

Orlando Boston Dallas Chicago San Diego

Visit *The Learning Site!*

www.harcourtschool.com

Bullfrog

Have you taken a walk in a meadow or by a pond? Did you hear something croak "CHUG-A-RUMM"?

If you hurried away, you may have missed something—a frog!

European Tree Frog

What Is a Frog?

What is a frog? It is an amphibian!

An amphibian is an animal that can live on land and in water. Many frogs live in or near water, but some live mostly on land. They may live in trees or in the ground.

Most frogs have long back legs and short front legs, or arms. Their skin takes in water. Frogs' skin must stay damp for them to live.

Frogs use their eyes to spot food—or enemies! They use their sticky tongues to catch insects.

Frogs "talk" by pulling air into their lungs and then pushing it out. CHUG-A-RUMM!

Kinds of Frogs

There are many kinds of frogs. A bullfrog is one of the biggest frogs. Some bullfrogs are seven inches long. Bullfrogs are good jumpers. They can jump about ten times as far as they are long!

bullfrog

Bullfrogs like to live in wet places. You might find them near ponds and lakes. They eat almost anything. They like fish, mice, small snakes—even other frogs!

green tree frog

Some frogs live in trees. A green tree frog is tiny but noisy. Perhaps one has cried "QUONK" near you!

Most tree frogs have sticky pads on their hands and feet. These help them cling to the tree when they climb.

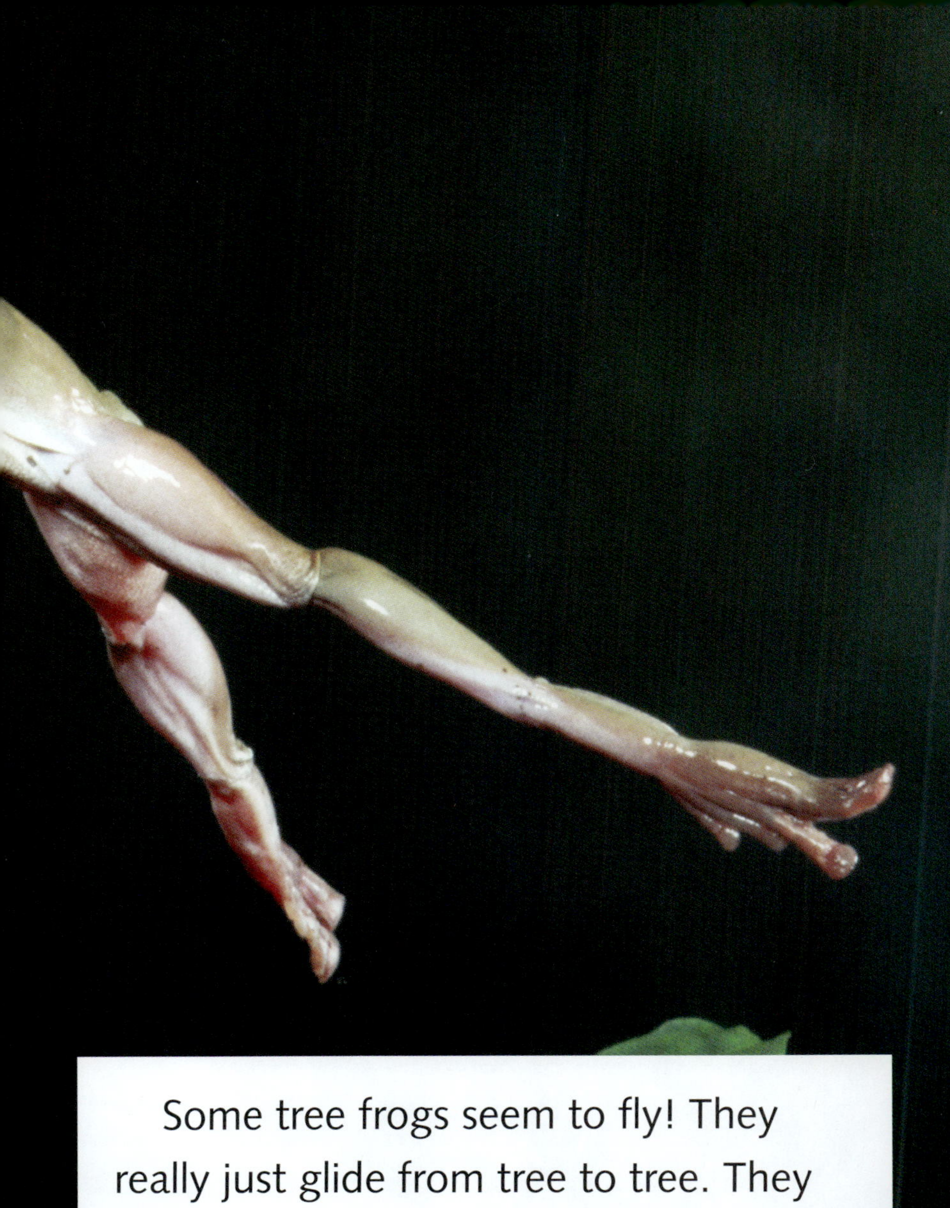

Some tree frogs seem to fly! They really just glide from tree to tree. They use their webbed hands and feet as brakes when they want to stop.

What Is a Toad?

Toads are amphibians too. They are like frogs in some ways but different in others.

Frogs have smooth skin. Toads have bumpy skin. Frogs have long back legs. Toads have short legs. Frogs like water. Toads like to live on land.

American toad

spadefoot toad

A spadefoot toad has thick arms and legs and webbed feet.

It has a hard "spade" on each foot—for a good reason. These toads dig burrows. They use their spades to do the digging!

horned toad

Toads like to eat bugs and this helps people. Garden and farm crops can be spoiled by insects. Toads and frogs eat some of these pesky insects.

cricket frog

Frogs and toads are fine little animals. If you hear "KICK-KICK-KICK," look around. That could be a cricket frog singing its note of cheer!

Index